Overheard on a Saltmarsh

POETS' FAVOURITE POEMS

Overheard on a Saltmarsh

POETS' FAVOURITE POEMS

Edited by
CAROL ANN DUFFY

YOUNG PICADOR

First published 2003
by Macmillan Children's Books
an imprint of Pan Macmillan Publishers Limited
20 New Wharf Road, London N1 9RR
Basingstoke and Oxford
www.panmacmillan.com

Associated companies throughout the world

ISBN 0 330 41556 5

1 3 5 7 9 8 6 4 2

A CIP catalogue record for this book is available from the British Library.
Printed by Mackays of Chatham plc, Chatham, Kent.

for Ella with love

CONTENTS

Introduction

The title for this anthology is taken from Harold Monro's luminously strange and wonderful poem which I've chosen to position, in pride of place, as the last poem here. *Overheard on a Saltmarsh* is among my favourite of those poems I know which favour the younger reader while still retaining the affection of the older. It thrilled and puzzled me as a child. As I got older, it got better. I read more into it. It gave me ideas. And now, as a poet who increasingly writes for children, I admire Monro's poem's passionate blend of innocence and knowingness, of sly, sensual humour and wide-eyed magic, of rhythm and voice. I love this poem as a reader and as a writer and have done all my life.

I thought I would invite poets whose work I enjoy – and whose poems are generous to younger readers as well as to older ones – to choose their favourite children's poem. In each case, a poem by the poet himself or herself appears alongside his or her choice. The present mingles with the past. Voices are raised, not hushed. Famous poems appear with a sudden draught of glamour. I knew that the poets here would choose not only childhood favourites, but poems that have stayed with them, that they continue to love and admire as poets as well as readers. A good poem from the past, to a living poet, can be like a torch found in a dark tunnel. It still has power. It works. It lights the way. The living poet can go on, further. I hope that reading this anthology will be like exploring a dark, jewelled cave with good guides.

Had I not had my heart set on *Overheard on a Saltmarsh* for my own choice, Marriott Edgar's *The Lion and Albert,* immortalised by Stanley Holloway's performance of it, would have been on my shortlist. Thankfully, Ken Smith has selected it. There are some poems that should be learned by heart at an early age and this is the top banana:

Then Pa, who had seen the occurrence,
  And didn't know what to do next,
Said 'Mother! Yon Lion's 'et Albert',
  And Mother said, 'Well I am vexed!'

Other favourites are here, welcome as a familiar song coming up on the jukebox. Adrian Mitchell had chosen *The Jumblies* by Edward Lear, one of the patron saints of children's poetry. Mitchell's own poem, *Back in the Playground Blues*, is a modern classic, a hip utterance of the darker side of growing up which anticipates rap by several decades. Lear, along with Walter de la Mare and Robert Louis Stevenson, has been chosen twice by the poets. Roger McGough, probably the most popular poet among young readers today, has chosen Edna St Vincent Millay's *Travel*. There is a clear and sympathetic echo between the two poets' styles:

All night there isn't a train goes by,
  Though the night is still for sleep and dreaming,
But I see its cinders red on the sky
  And hear its engine steaming.

The contemporary poets in this anthology range from the current Poet Laureate, Andrew Motion, to the performance poets Valerie Bloom and John Hegley; from best-selling poets like Wendy Cope (who selects a poem by her contemporary, Kit Wright) and Jenny Joseph to newcomers like Linda Chase and Amanda Dalton. In their own poems and in the poems they have chosen, they demonstrate that poetry is one place, that we first encounter it in childhood, and that its fruits and treasures stay in our minds as readers – and sometimes as writers – for a lifetime:

They are better than stars or water,
Better than voices of winds that sing,
Better than any man's fair daughter,
Your green glass beads on a silver ring.

CAROL ANN DUFFY

THE WORLD IS A BOX

My heart is a box of affection.
My head is a box of ideas.
My room is a box of protection.
My past is a box full of years.

The future's a box full of after.
An egg is a box full of yolk.
My life is a box full of laughter
And the world is a box full of folk.

SOPHIE HANNAH

WHOLE DUTY OF CHILDREN

A child should always say what's true,
And speak when he is spoken to,
And behave mannerly at table:
At least as far as he is able.

Robert Louis Stevenson
chosen by Sophie Hannah

THE SNAKE CATCHER SPEAKS

for Nachi

The best way to catch
           a northern water snake
is to corner it in a lake and let it
bite your arm — it will hold on tight
maintaining its grip
even as you raise your arm
           out of the water —

Of course, it hurts —
This snake has a large head,
a massive jaw, a mouth filled
with six rows of recurved teeth —
           And it will
                  defend itself —

But then you have it —
           There are ways
             to calm it.
After all, it is non-venomous
               Nerodia sipedon —
It is shy, elusive
           and only aggressive
when confronted.

2

Later,
          I always let it go –
after my students have watched it,
stared at it staring at them for months
          while they take notes –

I let it loose in the woods.
It is so fast – a sudden bolt
of energy – a black flash
darting out of my hands.

SUJATA BHATT

3

A SUMMER'S DREAM

To the sagging wharf
few ships could come.
The population numbered
two giants, an idiot, a dwarf,

a gentle storekeeper
asleep behind his counter,
and our kind landlady—
the dwarf was her dressmaker.

The idiot could be beguiled
by picking blackberries,
but then threw them away.
The shrunken seamstress smiled.

By the sea, lying
blue as a mackerel,
our boarding house was streaked
as though it had been crying.

Extraordinary geraniums
crowded the front windows,
the floors glittered with
assorted linoleums.

Every night we listened
for a horned owl.
In the horned lamp flame,
the wallpaper glistened.

The giant with the stammer
was the landlady's son,
grumbling on the stairs
over an old grammar.

He was morose,
but she was cheerful.
The bedroom was cold,
the feather bed close.

We were wakened in the dark by
the somnambulist brook
nearing the sea,
still dreaming audibly.

Elizabeth Bishop
chosen by Sujata Bhatt

Rain, Book, Classroom

A storm shades the page
like a stage light, dimmed,
rain hammers hard on roof-felted tin

and the children's cheeks
are bright as Christmas.
Down the soot-soft tunnels
of their fixed dark eyes,

down tracks as fine
as printed lines, black
on the blank winter fields
of the page, steam trains

to where we've never been:
a frontier town with one saloon,
a clapboard school
with stove smoke rising,

where a storm shades the page
like a stage light, dimmed, where
rain hammers hard on roof-felted tin.

Kate Clanchy

THE BLESSING

Just off the highway to Rochester, Minnesota,
Twilight bounds softly forth on the grass.
And the eyes of those two Indian ponies
Darken with kindness.
They have come gladly out of the willows
To welcome my friend and me.
We step over the barbed wire into the pasture
Where they have been grazing all day, alone.
They ripple tensely, they can hardly contain their happiness
That we have come.
They bow shyly as wet swans. They love each other.
There is no loneliness like theirs.
At home once more,
They begin munching the young tufts of spring in the darkness.
I would like to hold the slenderer one in my arms,
For she has walked over to me
And nuzzled my left hand.
She is black and white,
Her mane falls wild on her forehead,
And the light breeze moves me to caress her long ear
That is as delicate as the skin over a girl's wrist.
Suddenly I realize
That if I stepped out of my body I would break
Into blossom.

James Wright
chosen by Kate Clanchy

SECRET

Can you keep a secret?
Keep it in your mind,
Don't laugh, don't talk,
don't write it anywhere
In pen or chalk.

Ah tell me friend a secret,
Ah tell her not to tell,
Ah say is a special secret
So mek sure you keep it well.

Ah know dat it exciting,
But I asking you to try,
It would be bad if it get out,
So cross your heart and hope to die.

So ah tell me friend me secret,
From beginning to de end,
And that was de last o'dat secret,
She didn' even pretend

To keep it safe, she shout out,
In her loudes' voice,
'You mean you like that Malcolm?'
Now you tell me if dat nice?

She say she couldn' help it,
Say ah teck her by surprise,
Say ah really shoulda warn her.
Ah don't like to criticize

But when a person promise,
Take a oath right to your face,
She no ha' no right to broadcast
You business 'bout de place.

So ah ask me mum this morning,
Who can keep a secret most?
And she tell me, so me best friend
From now on is me bedpost.

VALERIE BLOOM

THE LISTENERS

'Is there anybody there?' said the Traveller,
Knocking on the moonlit door;
And his horse in the silence champed the grasses
Of the forest's ferny floor.
And a bird flew up out of the turret,
Above the Traveller's head:
And he smote upon the door again a second time;
'Is there anybody there?' he said.
But no one descended to the Traveller;
No head from the leaf-fringed sill
Leaned over and looked into his grey eyes,
Where he stood perplexed and still.
But only a host of phantom listeners
That dwelt in the lone house then
Stood listening in the quiet of the moonlight
To that voice from the world of men:
Stood thronging the faint moonbeams on the dark stair,
That goes down to the empty hall,
Hearkening in an air stirred and shaken
By the lonely Traveller's call.
And he felt in his heart their strangeness,
Their stillness answering his cry,
While his horse moved, cropping the dark turf,
'Neath the starred and leafy sky;
For he suddenly smote on the door, even
Louder, and lifted his head:—
'Tell them I came, and no one answered,
That I kept my word,' he said.
Never the least stir made the listeners,

Though every word he spake
Fell echoing through the shadowiness of the still house
From the one man left awake:
Ay, they heard his foot upon the stirrup,
And the sound of iron on stone,
And how the silence surged softly backward,
When the plunging hoofs were gone.

Walter de la Mare
chosen by Valerie Bloom

THE LUCKY ONES

Becky wore spectacles. Great big round ones
that made her eyes twice the size. *Smart*,
teacher said. It was the glasses.
I envied her and all the other lads and lassies.

Jason stayed after class to get help. Biscuits.
Cup of tea. *Special needs*, teacher said,
jolly Jason. But Miss, I said, what about me?
I've got needs, and I like tea.

Paul was tall, played basketball. Until he had a fall.
Broke his leg. But he didn't cry at all. Crutches.
And a smooth hard cast we autographed.
He didn't have to go to PE. Yes, but, what about me?

Sam had braces on his teeth, little rubber bands that
went bing when he laughed too hard or chewed bubble gum.
Perfect aim, his own special game.
He even knew how to spell orthodontist.

Lee, was stung by a bee. He was allergic.
Everyone ran and the ambulance too, whoop whooping
down the lane, a whirl of blurring light.
How I wished it had happened to me, stung by a bee.

Jennifer was pale as water, always taking her pills.
Brave little Jennifer, teacher said, *there there*,
using that soft voice, the way we talk to kittens.
Everyone had something that made them special.

If only something would happen to me, bang crash wallop.
I'd be as happy as a flea in fur. Spectacles, braces,
plaster cast, corrective boots, crutches, a scraped knee.
But nothing special ever happens to boring ole me.

JUDI BENSON

ADVENTURES OF ISABEL

Isabel met an enormous bear;
Isabel, Isabel, didn't care;
The bear was hungry, the bear was ravenous,
The bear's big mouth was cruel and cavernous.
The bear said, Isabel, glad to meet you,
How do, Isabel, now I'll eat you!
Isabel, Isabel, didn't worry,
Isabel didn't scream or scurry.
She washed her hands and she straightened her hair up,
Then Isabel quietly ate the bear up.

Once in a night as black as pitch
Isabel met a wicked old witch.
The witch's face was cross and wrinkled,
The witch's gums with teeth were sprinkled.
Ho ho, Isabel! the old witch crowed,
I'll turn you into an ugly toad!
Isabel, Isabel, didn't worry,
Isabel didn't scream or scurry.
She showed no rage and she showed no rancour,
But she turned the witch into milk and drank her.

Isabel met a hideous giant,
Isabel continued self-reliant.
The giant was hairy, the giant was horrid,
He had one eye in the middle of his forehead.
Good morning, Isabel, the giant said,
I'll grind your bones to make my bread.
Isabel, Isabel, didn't worry,

Isabel didn't scream or scurry.
She nibbled the zwieback that she always fed off,
And when it was gone, she cut the giant's head off.

Isabel met a troublesome doctor,
He punched and he poked till he really shocked her.
The doctor's talk was of coughs and chills
And the doctor's satchel bulged with pills.
And the doctor said unto Isabel,
Swallow this, it will make you well.
Isabel, Isabel, didn't worry,
Isabel didn't scream or scurry.
She took those pills from the pill concocter,
And Isabel calmly cured the doctor.

Ogden Nash
chosen by Judi Benson

An Attempt at Unrhymed Verse

People tell you all the time,
Poems do not have to rhyme.
It's often better if they don't
And I'm determined this one won't.
                              Oh dear.

Never mind, I'll start again.
Busy, busy with my pen . . . cil.
I can do it if I try –
Easy, peasy, pudding and gherkins.

Writing verse is so much fun,
Cheering as the summer weather,
Makes you feel alert and bright,
'Specially when you get it more or
        less the way you want it.

Wendy Cope

SONG SUNG BY A MAN ON A BARGE TO ANOTHER MAN ON A DIFFERENT BARGE IN ORDER TO DRIVE HIM MAD

Oh,

I am the best bargee bar none,
You are the best bargee bar one!
You are the second-best bargee,
You are the best bargee bar me!

Oh,

I am the best . . .

(and so on, until he is
hurled into the canal)

Kit Wright
chosen by Wendy Cope

17

TIMING

Two people at the seashore
being together
sharing the afternoon.

'Look, quick!
A flying fish!
Too bad,
You missed it.'

Couples go on like this.
One person even pretends
to see a shooting star.

'Look, quick!
A shooting star!
Too bad,
you missed it.'

LINDA CHASE

'ANYONE LIVED IN A PRETTY HOW TOWN . . .'

anyone lived in a pretty how town
(with up so floating many bells down)
spring summer autumn winter
he sang his didn't he danced his did.

Women and men(both little and small)
cared for anyone not at all
they sowed their isn't they reaped their same
sun moon stars rain

children guessed(but only a few
and down they forgot as up they grew
autumn winter spring summer)
that noone loved him more by more

when by now and tree by leaf
she laughed his joy she cried his grief
bird by snow and stir by still
anyone's any was all to her

someones married their everyones
laughed their cryings and did their dance
(sleep wake hope and then)they
said their nevers they slept their dream

stars rain sun moon
(and only the snow can begin to explain
how children are apt to forget to remember
with up so floating many bells down)

one day anyone died i guess
(and noone stooped to kiss his face)
busy folk buried them side by side
little by little and was by was

all by all and deep by deep
and more by more they dream their sleep
noone and anyone earth by april
wish by spirit and if by yes.

Women and men(both dong and ding)
summer autumn winter spring
reaped their sowing and went their came
sun moon stars rain

E. E. Cummings
chosen by Linda Chase

Wind Chimes

Here comes the wind.
It's winding your way.
Slates will be blown off,
Oak trees will sway.
Here comes the wind.

Here comes the wind.
At first it sounds soothing,
Then it gathers its voice
To a loud-mouthed booming.
Here comes the wind.

Here comes the wind.
An out-of-tune humming,
Backed with guitar
On the wires it is strumming.
Here comes the wind.

Here comes the wind.
Can't you tell it is itching
To slide down the chimney
And enter the kitchen?
Here comes the wind.

Here comes the wind.
People outdoors hold tight
To umbrellas and bus stops
In case they take flight.
Here comes the wind.

Here comes the wind.
It pounds and it clatters.
It bangs, thumps and beats.
It strikes, flogs and batters.
Here comes the wind.

Here comes the wind.
Nothing will stop it.
It seizes the dustbin,
Refuses to drop it.
Here comes the wind.

Here comes the wind.
Puffed full of cheek,
It calls out your name
But hides when you seek.
Here comes the wind.

Here comes the wind.
Now for its next stunt
It opens the back gate
And slams shut the front.
Here comes the wind.

Here comes the wind.
Yet it's not quite so strong:
It creates less of a roar
And more of a song.
There goes the wind.

There goes the wind.
A great calm descends.
Flowers pick themselves up
And everything mends.
There goes the wind.

There goes the wind.

Dennis O'Driscoll

23

The Diners in the Kitchen

Our dog Fred
Et the bread.

Our dog Dash
Et the hash.

Our dog Pete
Et the meat.

Our dog Davy
Et the gravy.

Our dog Toffy
Et the coffee.

Our dog Jake
Et the cake.

Our dog Trip
Et the dip.

And – the worst,
From the first, –

Our dog *Fi*do
Et the pie-dough.

James Whitcomb Riley
chosen by Dennis O'Driscoll

TOUCH

At Michael Cresswell's birthday party
we played *Statues*, *Twister*, *Kiss and Dare*
and, best of all, The Game Without A Name.

With blindfolds on, we shuffled round the table,
one by one, and someone pushed our fingers
into bowls of witches' bogeys,
hairy spider legs, and monster snot.

We weren't allowed to peep or lick or smell,
just touch.

I loved the shock of slime in the dark,
the shudder in my neck, the little scream,
as something cold and nasty slithered up my nails.

I didn't want to know that gouged-out eyes
were only hardboiled eggs in jelly,
or that alien killer insect spawn
was Co-op raspberry jam with seeds.

Susan Ranby did.
Before she'd even squeezed the werewolf's tongue
she threw up, everywhere,
and we were told to end the game.

She sat in the corner to wait for her mum.
Nobody'd touch her.

Amanda Dalton

A Dog in the Quarry

The day was so bright
    that even birdcages flew open.
The breasts of lawns
    heaved with joy
and the cars on the highway
    sang the great song of asphalt.
At Lobzy a dog fell in the quarry
    and howled.
Mothers pushed their prams out of the park opposite
because babies cannot sleep
    when a dog howls,
and a fat old pensioner was cursing the Municipality:
they let the dog fall in the quarry and then leave him there,
and this, if you please, has been going on since morning.

Towards evening even the trees
    stopped blossoming
and the water at the bottom of the quarry
    grew green with death.
But still the dog howled.

Then along came some boys
and made a raft out of two logs
and two planks.
And a man left on the bank
a briefcase, in which bread is planted
    in the morning

so that by noon
    crumbs may sprout in it
(the kind of briefcase in which documents
    and deeds
      would die of cramp),
he laid aside his briefcase
and sailed with them.

Their way led across a green puddle
to the island where the dog waited.
It was a voyage like
    the discovery of America,
a voyage like
    the quest of Theseus.
The dog fell silent,
    the boys stood like statues
and one of them punted with a stick,
the waves shimmered nervously,
tadpoles swiftly
    flickered out of the wake,
the heavens
    stood still,
and the man stretched out his hand.

  It was a hand
    reaching out across the ages,

it was a hand
    linking
    one world with another,
    life with death,
it was a hand
    joining everything together,
it caught the dog by the scruff of its neck

and then they sailed back
to the music of
an immense fanfare
of the dog's yapping.

It was not a question of that one dog.

It was not a question of that park.

Somehow it was a question
of our whole childhood,
    all of whose mischiefs
    will eventually out,
of all our loves,
of all the places we loved in
    and parted never to meet again,
of every prospect
    happy as grass,

unhappy as bone,
of every path up or down,
of every raft and all the other machines

we search for at our lathes
    and drawing-boards,
of everything we are reaching out for
round the corner of the landscape.

It was not an answer.

There are days when no answer is needed.

Miroslav Holub
chosen by Amanda Dalton

THE BEASTS

After the flood, they left the Ark.
(Two by two. Hurrah Hurrah Hurrah)
Noah had saved them. Life was good.
They mooed and roared their gratitude
(All together now. Hurrah Hurrah).

Noah had a vision of his sons
(One and two and three. Hurrah Hurrah)
A vision of fur and tusks and skins,
Of rifles, poison, harpoons, gins,
A whiff of battery hens (Hurrah Hurrah),

Draize-tested rabbits, cattle trucks,
(Thousands and thousands. Money for us. Hurrah)
Myxomatosis and abattoirs,
The pheasant shoot, the corrida
(Money and death. Hurrah Hurrah Hurrah).

Noah remembered the forty days
(The Arkful of precious lives. Hurrah Hurrah)
Tiger, panda, bittern, cod,
He knew how dear they were to God
(Who made them all. Hurrah Hurrah Hurrah).

He knelt down so the worms could hear
(No one counts worms. Hurrah Hurrah Hurrah)
He said, *You creatures great and small,*
My sons will soon destroy you all.
Scram! But they didn't scram nearly far
Enough.

(Hurrah

      Hurrah).

U. A. FANTHORPE

MUNICIPAL GUM

Gumtree in the city street,
Hard bitumen around your feet,
Rather you should be
In the cool world of leafy forest halls
And wild bird calls.
Here you seem to me
Like that poor cart-horse
Castrated, broken, a thing wronged,
Strapped and buckled, its hell prolonged,
Whose hung head and listless mien express
Its hopelessness.
Municipal gum, it is dolorous
To see you thus
Set in your black grass of bitumen –
O fellow citizen,
What have they done to us?

Kath Walker
chosen by U. A. Fanthorpe

IN A DARK STONE

'About seven thousand years ago
There was a little girl
Who looked in a mirror
And thought herself pretty.'

'I don't believe you. All that time ago
If there was a little girl she'd be wild
Wearing skins, and living in damp woods.'

'But seven thousand years ago
When England was a swamp with no one in it,
Long before the Romans,
In other lands by rivers and in plains
People made necklaces and learnt to write
And wrote down their accounts, and made fine pots,
Maps of the stars to sail by, and built cities;
And that is where they found this mirror
Where once the Hittite people roamed and ruled.'

'So you were there, were you, all that time ago
And living far from home in ancient Turkey?'

'No, but I saw this mirror. Here in England.
It was the smallest thing in a large hall
Of great bronze cauldrons, statues, slabs of stone.
You mustn't think that it was made of glass
Common, like our mirrors.   It was
A little lump of stone, shining; black; deep;
Hard like a thick black diamond, but better: obsidian.

It would have fitted in the palm of your hand.
One side was shaped and polished, the back rough.
Small though it was I crossed the room to see it.
I wanted to look in it, to see if it worked
Really, as a mirror, but I waited.'

'Why did you wait till nobody was round you?
You weren't trying to steal it were you?'
                                        'No. I was scared.

I waited and came slowly to it sideways.
I put my hand in front. It worked as a mirror.

And then I looked into that polished stone.
I thought the shadow of the shape I looked at
Was looking out at me. My face went into
That dark deep stone and joined the other face
The pretty one that used to search her mirror
When she was alive thousands of years ago.

I don't think she'd have come if there'd been a crowd.
They were all looking at the gold and brass.'

'I wish I could see it. Would she come for me?'

'I think the mirror's back in Turkey now.'

'I'd travel miles and miles if I could see it.'
'Well, nearer home, there were flint mines in Norfolk
And just where the land slopes a bit above some trees
On the Suffolk-Norfolk border, there's a track
And once I saw . . . But that's another story.'

JENNY JOSEPH

WHERE GO THE BOATS?

Dark brown is the river,
    Golden is the sand.
It flows along for ever,
    With trees on either hand.

Green leaves a-floating,
    Castles of the foam,
Boats of mine a-boating –
    Where will all come home?

On goes the river
    And out past the mill,
Away down the valley,
    Away down the hill.

Away down the river,
    A hundred miles or more,
Other little children
    Shall bring my boats ashore.

Robert Louis Stevenson
chosen by Jenny Joseph

RIDDLES

1. Take a field. Dry it. Mill it.
   Add a belly. Warm it. Fill it.

2. In bed together,
   you get bolder.
   Sadly, darling,
   I get colder.

3. White fence, pink hill,
   black valley, ruined mill.

4. Who's that knocking on my ring, says the chin.
   Me, says the stranger, I want to come in.

5. I would not saw the wood I see
   if what I saw was not a tree.

6. Onion, season, water's head
   share my name but not my bed.
   What am I that help you sleep
   yet feel as hard as bone of sheep?

7. Light as a light,
   tall as a house,
   the colour of angels,
   the voice of a mouse.

8. Who are we who never sit
   yet only work when we are hit?

9. Eat us little, eat us lots,
   rot your teeth and dot your spots.

10. Unwrap, my child,
    my squeaky shawl,
    and eat me, eat me,
    thorns and all.

11. Giant cow
    and giant queen,
    giant beet
    and giant bean,
    giant hand
    and giant mouth,
    giant North
    and giant South,
    giant throat
    and giant belly,
    giant beer
    and giant telly,
    giant bed
    and giant dream
    of giant drown
    in giant dream.

12. Poor little me,
    I get so bored –
    opened, squeezed,
    and then ignored.

SELIMA HILL
Answers on page 105

MEET-ON-THE-ROAD

'Now, pray, where are you going?' said Meet-on-the-Road.
'To school, sir, to school, sir,' said Child-as-it-Stood.

'What have you in your basket, child?' said Meet-on-the-Road.
'My dinner, sir, my dinner, sir,' said Child-as-it-Stood.

'What have you for dinner, child?' said Meet-on-the-Road.
'Some pudding, sir, some pudding sir,' said Child-as-it-Stood.

'Oh, then, I pray, give me a share,' said Meet-on-the-Road.
'I've little enough for myself, sir,' said Child-as-it-Stood.

'What have you got that cloak on for?' said Meet-on-the-Road.
'To keep the wind and cold from me,' said Child-as-it-Stood.

'I wish the wind would blow through you,' said Meet-on-
    the-Road.
'Oh, what a wish! What a wish!' said Child-as-it-Stood.

'Pray, what are those bells ringing for?' said Meet-on-the-Road.
'To bring bad spirits home again,' said Child-as-it-Stood.

'Oh, then I must be going child!' said Meet-on-the-Road.
'So fare you well, so fare you well,' said Child-as-it-Stood.

Anon.
chosen by Selima Hill

HISTORY LESSON

First, one
in the crowd puts the eye on you –
a nod to number two

who gets the message
and flips back something side-
long, something snide

that everybody hears
but you. Soon three or four
are in it. They'll make sure

you catch the steel
glint of the snigger they wear
like a badge. And there

come five or six
together, casual, shouldering in
around you with a single grin

and nothing you say
seems to reach them at all.
The badmouthings they call

mean only this:
they want to scratch. You are the itch.
A thousand years stand by, hissing *Witch!*

Nigger! Yid!
All you hear is silence lumbered
shut around you. And the ten or hundred

  looking on
look on. They are learning not to see.
The bell rings, too late. Already

this is history.

PHILIP GROSS

I Saw a Jolly Hunter

I saw a jolly hunter
    With a jolly gun
Walking in the country
    In the jolly sun.

In the jolly meadow
    Sat a jolly hare.
Saw the jolly hunter.
    Took jolly care.

Hunter jolly eager –
    Sight of jolly prey.
Forgot gun pointing
    Wrong jolly way.

Jolly hunter jolly head
    Over heels gone.
Jolly old safety catch
    Not jolly on.

Bang went the jolly gun.
    Hunter jolly dead.
Jolly hare got clean away.
    Jolly good, I said.

Charles Causley
chosen by Philip Gross

THE DRAGONFLY

There was once a terrible monster
lived in a pond, deep under the water.

Brown as mud he was, in the mud he hid,
among murk of reed-roots, sodden twigs,
with his long hungry belly,
six legs for creeping,
eyes like headlights
awake or sleeping;
but he was not big.

A tiddler came to sneer and jeer
and flaunt his flashing tail—
Ugly old stick-in-the-mud
couldn't catch a snail!
I'm not scared—
when, like a shot,
two pincers nab him, and he's got!

For the monster's jaw hides a clawed stalk
like the arm of a robot, a dinner fork,
that's tucked away cunningly till the last minute—
shoots out—and back with a victim in it!

Days, weeks, months, two years and beyond,
fear of the monster beset the pond;
he lurked, grabbed, grappled, gobbled and grew,
ambushing always somewhere new—

Who saw him last? Does anyone know?
Don't go near the mud! But I must go!
Keep well away from the rushes! But how?
Has anyone seen my sister? Not for a week now—
she's been eaten
for certain!

And then, one day, it was June, they all saw him.
He was coming slowly up out of the mud,
they stopped swimming. No one dared
approach, attack. They kept back.

Up a tall reed they saw him climbing
higher and higher, until
he broke the surface, climbing still.

There he stopped, in the wind and the setting sun.
We're safe at last! they cried. *He's gone!*

What became of the monster, was he ill, was he sad?
Was nobody sorry? Had he crept off to die? Was he mad?

Not one of them saw how, suddenly,
as if an invisible knife had touched his back,
he has split, split completely—
his head split like a lid!
The cage is open. Slowly he comes through,
an emperor, with great eyes burning blue.

He rests there, veils of silver a cloak for him.
Night and the little stars travel the black pond,
and now, first light of the day,
his shining cloak wide wings, a flash, a whirr,
a jewelled helicopter,
he's away!

O fully he had served his time,
shunned and unlovely in the drab slime,
for freedom at the end—for the sky—
dazzling hunter, Dragonfly!

LIBBY HOUSTON

CALICO PIE

I

Calico Pie,
  The little Birds fly
Down to the calico tree,
    Their wings were blue,
    And they sang 'Tilly-loo!'
    Till away they flew,—
And they never came back to me!
    They never came back!
    They never came back!
They never came back to me!

Calico Jam,
  The little Fish swam
Over the syllabub sea,
    He took off his hat,
    To the Sole and the Sprat,
    And the Willeby-wat,—
But he never came back to me!
    He never came back!
    He never came back!
He never came back to me!

III

Calico Ban,
The little Mice ran,
To be ready in time for tea,
Flippity flup,
They drank it all up,
And danced in the cup,—
But they never came back to me!
They never came back!
They never came back!
They never came back to me!

IV

Calico Drum,
The Grasshoppers come,
The Butterfly, Beetle, and Bee,
Over the ground,
Around and round,
With a hop and a bound,—
But they never came back!
They never came back!
They never came back!
They never came back to me!

Edward Lear
chosen by Libby Houston

EDDIE DON'T LIKE FURNITURE

Eddie don't go for sofas or settees
or those little tables that you have to buy in threes
the closest thing that Eddie's got to an article of
    furniture's
the cheese board
Eddie doesn't bolster the upholstery biz
there's a lot of furniture in the world but none of it's
    Eddie's
he won't have it in the house however well it's made
Eddie's bedroom was fully furnished
when the floorboards had been laid
and Eddie played guitar
until he decided that his guitar was far too like
an article of furniture
Eddie offers visitors a corner of the room
you get used to the distances between you pretty soon
but with everyone in corners though
it isn't very easy when you're trying to play pontoon
he once got in a rowing boat and they offered him a
    seat
it was just a strip of timber but it wasn't up his street
he stood himself up in the boat and made himself feel
    steady
then he threw the plank on to the bank and said
furniture?
no thank you
when it's on a bonfire furniture's fine
any time that Eddie gets a number twenty-nine bus
even if there's seats on top and plenty down below

Eddie always goes where the pushchairs go
does Eddie like furniture?
I don't think so
if you go round Eddie's place and have a game of
    hide and seek
it isn't very long before you're found
and in a fit of craziness Eddie took the legs off his dash
    hound
that stopped him dashing around
Eddie quite likes cutlery
but he don't like furniture
if you give him some for Christmas
he'll returniture

JOHN HEGLEY

TARANTELLA

Do you remember an Inn,
Miranda?
Do you remember an Inn?
And the tedding and the spreading
Of the straw for a bedding,
And the fleas that tease in the High Pyrenees,
And the wine that tasted of the tar?
And the cheers and the jeers of the young muleteers
(Under the vine of the dark verandah)?
Do you remember an Inn, Miranda,
Do you remember an Inn?
And the cheers and the jeers of the young muleteers
Who hadn't got a penny,
And who weren't paying any,
And the hammer at the doors and the Din?
And the Hip! Hop! Hap!
Of the clap
Of the hands to the twirl and the swirl
Of the girl gone chancing,
Glancing,
Dancing,
Backing and advancing,
Snapping of a clapper to the spin
Out and in –
And the Ting, Tong, Tang of the Guitar!
Do you remember an Inn,
Miranda?
Do you remember an Inn!

Never more;
Miranda,
Never more.
Only the high peaks hoar:
And Aragon a torrent at the door.
No sound
In the walls of the Halls where falls
The tread
Of the feet of the dead to the ground
No sound:
But the boom
Of the far Waterfall like Doom.

Hilaire Belloc
chosen by John Hegley

THE WORLD OF TREES

Sycamore. Mountain Ash. Beech. Birch. Oak.

In the middle of the forest the trees stood.
And the beech knew the birch was there.
And the mountain ash breathed the same air
as the sycamore, and everywhere

the wind blew, the trees understood each other:
how the river made the old oak lean to the east,
how the felled beech changed the currents of the wind,
how the two common ash formed a canopy

and grew in a complementary way.
Between them they shared a full head of hair.
Some amber curls of the one could easily
belong to the other: twin trees, so similar.

Sycamore. Mountain Ash. Beech. Birch. Oak.

Some trees crouched in the forest, waiting
for another tree to die so that they could
shoot up suddenly in that new space,
stretch out comfortably for the blue sky.

Some trees grew mysterious mushroom fungi,
shoelace, honey, intricate as a grandmother's lace.
The wind fluttered the leaves; the leaves flapped their wings.
Birds flew from the trees. Sometimes they'd sing.

The tall trees, compassionate, understood everything:
Grief – they stood stock still, branches drooped in despair.
Fear – they exposed their many roots, tugged their gold hair.
Anger – they shook in the storm, pointed their bony fingers.

Sycamore. Mountain Ash. Beech. Birch. Oak.

The trees knew each other's secrets.
In the deep green heart of the forest,
each tree loved another tree best.
Each tree, happy to rest, leans a little to the east

or to the west, when the moon loomed high above,
the big white eye of the woods.
And they stood together as one in the dark,
with the stars sparkling from their branches,

completely at ease, breathing in the cold night air.
Swishing a little in the breeze,
dreaming of glossy spring leaves
in the fine distinguished company of trees.

Sycamore. Mountain Ash. Beech. Birch. Oak.

JACKIE KAY

WILLIE'S WIFE

Willie Wastle dwalt on Tweed,
The spot they ca'd it Linkumdoddie;
Willie was a wabster guid,
Cou'd stown a clue wi' ony body.
He had a wife was dour and din,
O Tinkler Madgie was her mither;
Sic a wife as Willie had,
He wad na gie a button for her!

She was an ee, she has but ane,
The cat has twa the very colour:
Five rusty teeth, forbye a stump,
A clapper tongue was deave a miller;
A whiskin beard about her mou,
Her nose and chin they threaten ither;
Sic a wife as Willie had,
He wad na gie a button for her!

She's a bow-hough'd, she's hein shinn'd,
Ae limpin leg a hand-breed shorter;
She's twisted right, she's twisted left,
To balance fair in ilka quarter:
She has a hump upon a breast,
The twin o' that upon her shouther;
Sic a wife as Willie had,
He wad na gie a button for her!

Auld baudrons by the ingle sits,
An' wi' her loof her face a-washin;
But Willie's wife is nae sae trig,
She dights her grunzle wi' a hushion;
Her walie nieves like midden-creels,
Her face wad fyle the Logan-water;
Sic a wife as Willie had,
I wad na gie a button for her!

Robert Burns
chosen by Jackie Kay

MOON-GAZER

On moonlight night
when moon is bright
Beware, Beware —

Moon-Gazer man
with his throw-back head
and his open legs
gazing, gazing
up at the moon

Moon-Gazer man
with his seal-skin hair
and his round-eye stare
staring, staring
up at the moon.

Moon-Gazer man
standing tall,
lamp-post tall,
just gazing up
at moon eye-ball

But never try to pass
between those open legs
cause Moon-Gazer man
will close them with a snap —
you'll be trapped

Moon-Gazer man
will crush you flat.
Yes, with just one shake
suddenly you'll be –
a human pancake

On moonlight night
when moon is bright
for goodness' sake
stay home –
and pull your window-curtain tight.

('Moon-Gazer' is a supernatural folk-figure, extremely tall, who could be seen mostly straddling roadways on moonlit nights, gazing up at the moon. It is best to avoid passing between his legs.)

GRACE NICHOLS

MILLIONS OF STRAWBERRIES

Marcia and I went over the curve,
Eating our way down
Jewels of strawberries we didn't deserve,
Eating our way down,
Till our hands were sticky, and our lips painted.
And over us the hot day fainted,
And we saw snakes,
And got scratched,
And a lust overcame us for the red unmatched
Small buds of berries,
Till we lay down—
Eating our way down—
And rolled in the berries like two little dogs,
Rolled
In the late gold.
And gnats hummed,
And it was cold,
And home we went, home without a berry,
Painted red and brown,
Eating our way down.

Genevieve Taggard
chosen by Grace Nichols

Robinson Crusoe's Wise Sayings

You can never have too many turtle's eggs.
I'm the most interesting person in this room.
A beard is as long as I want it to be.

The swimmer on his own doesn't need trunks.
A tree is a good clock.
If you talk to a stone long enough you'll fall asleep.

I know it's Christmas because I cry.
Waving at ships is useless.
Footprints make me happy, unless they're my own.

Ian McMillan

Hamnavoe Market

They drove to the market with ringing pockets.

Folster found a girl
Who put wounds on his face and throat,
Small and diagonal, like red doves.

Johnston stood by the barrel.
All day he stood there.
He woke in a ditch, his mouth full of ashes.

Grieve bought a balloon and a goldfish.
He swung through the air.
He fired shotguns, rolled pennies, ate sweet fog from a stick.

Heddle was at the market also.
I know nothing of his activities.
He is and always was a quiet man.

Garson fought three rounds with a negro boxer,
And received thirty shillings,
Much applause, and an eye loaded with thunder.

Where did they find Flett?
They found him in a brazen circle,
All flame and blood, a new salvationist.

A gypsy saw in the hand of Halcro
Great strolling herds, harvests, a proud woman.
He wintered in the poorhouse.

They drove home from the market under the stars
Except for Johnston
Who lay in a ditch, his mouth full of dying fires.

George Mackay Brown
chosen by Ian McMillan

To Whom it May Concern

This poem about ice cream
has nothing to do with government,
with riot, with any political scheme.

It is a poem about ice cream. You see?
About how you might stroll into a shop
and ask: *One Strawberry Split. One Mivvi.*

What did I tell you? No one will die.
No licking tongues will melt like candle wax.
This is a poem about ice cream. Do not cry.

Andrew Motion

WARNING TO CHILDREN

Children, if you dare to think
Of the greatness, rareness, muchness,
Fewness of this precious only
Endless world in which you say
You live, you think of things like this:
Blocks of slate enclosing dappled
Red and green, enclosing tawny
Yellow nets, enclosing white
And black acres of dominoes,
Where a neat brown paper parcel
Tempts you to untie the string.
In the parcel a small island,
On the island a large tree,
On the tree a husky fruit.
Strip the husk and pare the rind off:
In the kernel you will see
Blocks of slate enclosed by dappled
Red and green, enclosed by tawny
Yellow nets, enclosed by white
And black acres of dominoes,
Where the same brown paper parcel—
Children, leave the string alone!
For who dares undo the parcel
Finds himself at once inside it,
On the island, in the fruit,
Blocks of slate about his head,
Finds himself enclosed by dappled
Green and red, enclosed by yellow
Tawny nets, enclosed by black

And white acres of dominoes,
With the same brown paper parcel
Still unopened on his knee.
And, if he then should dare to think
Of the fewness, muchness, rareness,
Greatness of this endless only
Precious world in which he says
He lives—he then unties the string.

Robert Graves
chosen by Andrew Motion

BACK IN THE PLAYGROUND BLUES

I dreamed I was back in the playground, I was about
    four feet high
Yes, dreamed I was back in the playground, standing about
    four feet high
Well the playground was three miles long and the
    playground was five miles wide

It was broken black tarmac with a high wire fence all round
Broken black dusty tarmac with a high fence running
    all around
And it had a special name to it, they called it
    The Killing Ground

Got a mother and a father, they're one thousand years away
The rulers of The Killing Ground are coming out to play
Everybody thinking: 'Who they going to play with today?'

    Well you get it for being Jewish
    And you get it for being black
    Get it for being chicken
    And you get it for fighting back
    You get it for being big and fat
    Get it for being small
    Oh those who get it get it and get it
    For any damn thing at all

Sometimes they take a beetle, tear off its six legs one by one
Beetle on its black back, rocking in the lunchtime sun
But a beetle can't beg for mercy, a beetle's not half the fun

I heard a deep voice talking, it had that iceberg sound
'It prepares them for Life' – but I have never found
Any place in my life worse than The Killing Ground.

ADRIAN MITCHELL

THE JUMBLIES

I

They went to sea in a Sieve, they did,
    In a Sieve they went to sea:
In spite of all their friends could say,
On a winter's morn, on a stormy day,
    In a Sieve they went to sea!
And when the Sieve turned round and round,
And every one cried, 'You'll all be drowned!'
They called aloud, 'Our Sieve ain't big,
But we don't care a button! we don't care a fig!
    In a Sieve we'll go to sea!'
      Far and few, far and few,
        Are the lands where the Jumblies live;
        Their heads are green, and their hands are blue,
        And they went to sea in a Sieve.

II

They sailed away in a Sieve, they did,
    In a Sieve they sailed so fast,
With only a beautiful pea-green veil
Tied with a riband by way of a sail,
    To a small tobacco-pipe mast;
And every one said, who saw them go,
'O won't they be soon upset, you know!
For the sky is dark, and the voyage is long,
And happen what may, it's extremely wrong

In a Sieve to sail so fast!'
      Far and few, far and few,
          Are the lands where the Jumblies live;
      Their heads are green, and their hands are blue,
          And they went to sea in a Sieve.

III

The water it soon came in, it did,
    The water it soon came in;
So to keep them dry, they wrapped their feet
In a pinky paper all folded neat,
    And they fastened it down with a pin.
And they passed the night in a crockery-jar,
And each of them said, 'How wise we are!
Though the sky be dark, and the voyage be long,
Yet we never can think we were rash or wrong,
    While round in our Sieve we spin!'
      Far and few, far and few,
          Are the lands where the Jumblies live;
      Their heads are green, and their hands are blue,
          And they went to sea in a Sieve.

IV

And all night long they sailed away;
    And when the sun went down,
They whistled and warbled a moony song

To the echoing sound of a coppery gong,
    In the shade of the mountains brown.
'O Timballo! How happy we are,
When we live in a sieve and a crockery-jar,
And all night long in the moonlight pale,
We sail away with a pea-green sail,
    In the shade of the mountains brown!'
        Far and few, far and few,
            Are the lands where the Jumblies live;
        Their heads are green, and their hands are blue,
            And they went to sea in a Sieve.

V

They sailed to the Western Sea, they did,
    To a land all covered with trees,
And they bought an Owl, and a useful Cart,
And a pound of Rice, and a Cranberry Tart,
    And a hive of silvery Bees.
And they bought a Pig, and some green Jack-daws,
And a lovely Monkey with lollipop paws,
And forty bottles of Ring-Bo-Ree,
    And no end of Stilton Cheese.
        Far and few, far and few,
            Are the lands where the Jumblies live;
        Their heads are green, and their hands are blue,
            And they went to sea in a Sieve.

VI

And in twenty years they all came back,
   In twenty years or more,
And every one said, 'How tall they've grown!
For they've been to the Lakes, and the Torrible Zone,
   And the hills of the Chankly Bore';
And they drank their health, and gave them a feast
Of dumplings made of beautiful yeast;
And every one said, 'If we only live,
We too will go to sea in a Sieve,—
   To the hills of the Chankly Bore!'
     Far and few, far and few,
      Are the lands where the Jumblies live;
     Their heads are green, and their hands are blue,
      And they went to sea in a Sieve.

Edward Lear
chosen by Adrian Mitchell

THE MIDNIGHT SKATERS

It is midnight in the ice-rink
    And all is cool and still.
Darkness seems to hold its breath
    Nothing moves, until

Out of the kitchen, one by one,
    The cutlery comes creeping,
Quiet as mice to the brink of the ice
    While all the world is sleeping.

Then suddenly, a serving-spoon
    Switches on the light,
And the silver swoops upon the ice
    Screaming with delight.

The knives are high-speed skaters
    Round and round they race,
Blades hissing, sissing,
    Whizzing at a dizzy pace.

Forks twirl like dancers
    Pirouetting on the spot.
Teaspoons (who take no chances)
    Hold hands and giggle a lot.

All night long the fun goes on
    Until the sun, their friend,
Gives the warning signal
    That all good things must end.

So they slink back to the darkness
Of the kitchen cutlery-drawer
And steel themselves to wait
Until it's time to skate once more.

*

At eight the canteen ladies
Breeze in as good as gold
To lay the tables and wonder
Why the cutlery is so cold.

ROGER McGOUGH

TRAVEL

The railroad track is miles away,
    And the day is loud with voices speaking,
Yet there isn't a train goes by all day
    But I hear its whistle shrieking.

All night there isn't a train goes by,
    Though the night is still for sleep and dreaming
But I see its cinders red on the sky
    And hear its engine steaming.

My heart is warm with the friends I make,
    And better friends I'll not be knowing,
Yet there isn't a train I wouldn't take,
    No matter where it's going.

Edna St Vincent Millay
chosen by Roger McGough

Paper Boat

Make a little paper boat,
Take it to the river,
If it swims and stays afloat,
You will live forever.

Gerda Mayer

Rondeau

Jenny kissed me when we met,
    Jumping from the chair she sat in;
Time, you thief, who love to get
    Sweets into your list, put that in!
Say I'm weary, say I'm sad,
    Say that health and wealth have missed me,
Say I'm growing old, but add,
    Jenny kissed me.

James Leigh Hunt
chosen by Gerda Mayer

SISTER IN A WHALE

You live in the hollow of a stranded whale
lying on top of our house.
My father was embarrassed by this
so a roof was put up as camouflage.
On the ribs you have hung plants
and a miniature replica of a whale
to remind you where you are.
The stomach lining is plastered with posters
and your *Snoopy for President* buttons
are stuck to a piece of blubber beside your bed.
Through the spout you observe cloud formations.
It isn't as orderly as a regular room:
it's more like a shipwreck of notebooks,
school projects, shirts, paper bags,
coke cans, photographs and magazines
that has been washed up with the tide.
You beachcomb every morning for something to wear;
then it's down the corkscrew
to the real world.

JULIE O'CALLAGHAN

Hunter Trials

It's awfully bad luck on Diana,
    Her ponies have swallowed their bits;
She fished down their throats with a spanner
    And frightened them all into fits.

So now she's attempting to borrow
    Do lend her some bits, Mummy, *do*;
I'll lend her my own for tomorrow,
    But today *I*'ll be wanting them too.

Just look at Prunella on Guzzle,
    The wizardest pony on earth;
Why doesn't she slacken his muzzle
    And tighten the breech in his girth?

I say, Mummy, there's Mrs Geyser
    And doesn't she look pretty sick?
I bet it's because Mona Lisa
    Was hit on the hock with a brick.

Miss Blewitt says Monica threw it,
    But Monica says it was Joan,
And Joan's very thick with Miss Blewitt,
    So Monica's sulking alone.

And Margaret failed in her paces,
    Her withers got tied in a noose,
So her coronets caught in the traces
    And now all her fetlocks are loose.

Oh, it's me now. I'm terribly nervous.
   I wonder if Smudges will shy.
She's practically certain to swerve as
   Her Pelham is over one eye.

*

Oh wasn't it naughty of Smudges?
   Oh, Mummy, I'm sick with disgust.
She threw me in front of the Judges,
   And my silly old collarbone's bust.

John Betjeman
chosen by Julie O'Callaghan

PETS

When I was in the Infants I pinched
the school's goldfish. I felt sorry for them,
one tiny meal a day, not much water,
swimming in circles watching us do sums;
I decided to free them in the canal.

My mate Mitch hid with me after school
in the cloakroom, pretending to be
looking for a coat when the cleaner came;
after she'd gone we raided our classroom
for the bowl. The canal was a long way;

We were walking really slow, trying not
to slop the water when we met Mrs Sparks
the school secretary who demanded to know
where we were going. 'Taking these fish home.
An old man was giving them away as pets.'

But she recognized the bowl, ordered us
to carry them back. Afterwards they bought
a proper aquarium to keep the fish healthy
so we rescued the guinea pig. He had
a great time with us before they found out.

IRENE RAWNSLEY

HUMPTY DUMPTY'S POEM
from *Through the Looking-Glass*

In winter, when the fields are white,
I sing this song for your delight—

*

In spring, when woods are getting green,
I'll try and tell you what I mean.

*

In summer, when the days are long,
Perhaps you'll understand the song:

In autumn, when the leaves are brown,
Take pen and ink and write it down.

*

I sent a message to the fish:
I told them 'This is what I wish.'

The little fishes of the sea,
They sent an answer back to me.

The little fishes' answer was
'We cannot do it, Sir, because—'

*

I sent to them again to say
'It will be better to obey.'

The fishes answered with a grin,
'Why, what a temper you are in!'

I told them once, I told them twice:
They would not listen to advice.

I took a kettle large and new,
Fit for the deed I had to do.

My heart went hop, my heart went thump:
I filled the kettle at the pump.

Then someone came to me and said,
'The little fishes are in bed.'

I said to him, I said it plain,
'Then you must wake them up again.'

I said it very loud and clear;
I went and shouted in his ear.

*

But he was very stiff and proud;
He said 'You needn't shout so loud!'

And he was very proud and stiff;
He said 'I'd go and wake them if—'

I took a corkscrew from the shelf:
I went to wake them up myself.

And when I found the door was locked,
I pulled and pushed and kicked and knocked.

And when I found the door was shut,
I tried to turn the handle, but—

Lewis Carroll
chosen by Irene Rawnsley

BURYING MOSES

Moses was very old,
Ninety-eight, my grandpa said,
So we shouldn't cry too much
Now poor old Moses was dead.

Moses used to be black
But he slowly turned grey as a fog,
And snuffled and wheezed and snored.
Moses was our old dog.

Each year that people live
Counts for a dog as seven.
'He was a good old boy,' said Grandpa,
'He's sure to go to heaven.

'But first we must go and bury him
At the back of the garden shed,
So come and give me a hand;
We'll make him a deep warm bed.'

And so we lowered old Moses
Down in the hole Grandpa dug,
And he huddled there in a bundle
Like a dusty old fireside rug.

Then we filled in the hole and patted
The soil down smooth and flat.
'I'll make him a cross,' said Grandpa.
'The least we can do is that.

'He'll be wagging his tail in heaven,
So you mustn't be too upset . . . '
But Grandpa's voice sounded croaky,
And I could see his old cheeks were wet.

VERNON SCANNELL

Stopping by Woods on a Snowy Evening

Whose woods these are I think I know.
His house is in the village though;
He will not see me stopping here
To watch his woods fill up with snow.

My little horse must think it queer
To stop without a farmhouse near
Between the woods and frozen lake
The darkest evening of the year.

He gives his harness bells a shake
To ask if there is some mistake.
The only other sound's the sweep
Of easy wind and downy flake.

The woods are lovely, dark and deep,
But I have promises to keep,
And miles to go before I sleep,
And miles to go before I sleep.

Robert Frost
chosen by Vernon Scannell

THE RED HOUSE

sits in the elm tree
like a nest –
a square, red nest
made of wood.

It would float away if it could.

Its one window
faces north,
the dangerous north.
It has no door –

just a square hold in the floor.

Who lives there?
A monkey,
a red monkey
with no tail –

like a yacht without a sail.

And every evening
a boy,
a blond boy
stands below

to shout into the tree HELLO.

But the monkey
stares down,
scowls down
and won't descend.

He's not the boy's friend.

He was once
when his house,
his red house,
was built.

Now he smells the boy's guilt

that wafts up
to join the pain,
the phantom pain
in his tail.

And the monkey starts to wail

sending the boy
marching home,
running home
like a mouse

while the sun sets on the red house.

MATTHEW SWEENEY

JOHN MOULDY

I spied John Mouldy in his cellar,
Deep down twenty steps of stone;
In the dusk he sat a-smiling,
    Smiling there alone.

He read no book, he snuffed no candle;
The rats ran in, the rats ran out;
And far and near, the drip of water
    Went whisp'ring about.

The dusk was still, with dew a-falling,
I saw the Dog-star bleak and grim,
I saw a slim brown rat of Norway
    Creep over him.

I spied John Mouldy in his cellar,
Deep down twenty steps of stone;
In the dusk he sat a-smiling,
    Smiling there alone.

Walter de la Mare
chosen by Matthew Sweeney

KATJA'S MESSAGE:

'This sentence has no meaning,
but what are you going to do about the crocodiles?'

In Berlin, attempting sleep, this sentence
without meaning keeping me awake;
one by one the hours climb the clock,
labour as slowly down the other side.

The silence at the border is absolute,
full of watching darkness, wire and neon,
the dark trees either side without wind
or weather or the baying of dogs.

It goes on and on, the silence, a lake
without a name where legends surface:
a bead of air, a log of wood, a skin,
an eye blinked open in the dark.

It is the crocodile, easing down
into another sleepless night
along the border, here beside the wall,
where still this sentence has no meaning.

KEN SMITH

The Lion and Albert

There's a famous seaside place called Blackpool,
    That's noted for fresh air and fun,
And Mr and Mrs Ramsbottom
    Went there with young Albert, their son.

A grand little lad was young Albert,
    All dressed in his best; quite a swell
With a stick with an 'orse's 'ead 'andle,
    The finest that Woolworth's could sell.

They didn't think much to the Ocean:
    The waves, they was fiddlin' and small,
There was no wrecks and nobody drownded,
    Fact, nothing to laugh at at all.

So, seeking for further amusement,
    They paid and went into the Zoo,
Where they'd Lions and Tigers and Camels,
    And old ale and sandwiches too.

There were one great big Lion called Wallace;
    His nose were all covered with scars –
He lay in a somnolent posture,
    With the side of his face on the bars.

Now Albert had heard about Lions,
     How they was ferocious and wild –
To see Wallace lying so peaceful,
     Well, it didn't seem right to the child.

So straightway the brave little feller,
     Not showing a morsel of fear,
Took his stick with its 'orse's 'ead 'andle
. . . And pushed it in Wallace's ear.

You could see that the Lion didn't like it,
     For giving a kind of a roll,
He pulled Albert inside the cage with 'im,
     And swallowed the little lad 'ole.

Then Pa, who had seen the occurrence,
     And didn't know what to do next,
Said 'Mother! Yon Lion's 'et Albert',
     And Mother said, 'Well I am vexed!'

Then Mr and Mrs Ramsbottom –
     Quite rightly, when all's said and done –
Complained to the Animal Keeper,
     That the Lion had eaten their son.

The keeper was quite nice about it;
    He said 'What a nasty mishap.
Are you sure that it's *your* boy he's eaten?'
    Pa said 'Am I sure? There's his cap!'

The manager had to be sent for.
    He came and he said 'What's to do?'
Pa said 'Yon Lion's 'et Albert,
    And 'im in his Sunday clothes, too.'

Then Mother said, 'Right's right, young feller;
    I think it's a shame and a sin,
For a lion to go and eat Albert,
    And after we've paid to come in.'

The manager wanted no trouble,
    He took out his purse right away,
Saying 'How much to settle the matter?'
    And Pa said 'What do you usually pay?'

But Mother had turned a bit awkward
    When she thought where her Albert had gone.
She said 'No! someone's got to be summonsed' –
    So that was decided upon.

Then off they went to the P'lice Station,
    In front of the Magistrate chap;
They told 'im what happened to Albert,
    And proved it by showing his cap.

The Magistrate gave his opinion
    That no one was really to blame
And he said that he hoped the Ramsbottoms
    Would have further sons to their name.

At that Mother got proper blazing,
    'And thank you, sir, kindly,' said she.
'What waste all our lives raising children
    To feed ruddy Lions? Not me!'

Marriott Edgar
chosen by Ken Smith

KINGS OF THE PLAYGROUND

All to get the Bully – who hid in a steel-clad cupboard –
The Bully Bashers stormed the trembling school.
They bullied the Bully's kit, his grubby blazer,
his sports-bag, his bully-beef flavour crisps.

They bullied the kids with the bruises
that showed the Bully's shoe-print.
They bullied the gerbils he'd teased, they bullied every
    computer
he'd slimed with his bully virus.

They bullied the prefects and teachers –
the nice ones first, then the bullies.
The kids who had conduct stars, the kids in detention, even
the football team, they bullied, yelling, 'Ya bullying fairies!'

They bullied the books, though the Bully didn't like books:
they bullied the white boards and black-boards,
they bullied the wall-charts, the registers, the sick-notes,
the pass-notes. They bullied the two times table.

Then they thundered out and bullied the empty playground,
they bullied the big round sky that covered the playground,
they bullied the rain, the bushes, the used needles,
the trembling waiting parents, the tiny brothers and sisters.

Bully TV was launched. There was only one programme
'How We Bashed the Bully.' Anyone who switched off
Was sentenced to 25 years community-bullying.
The Bully Bashers relaxed. Gave themselves medals.
    Flew home.

The Bully listened a while, and grinned in the dark
    cupboard.
Then he combed his hair and opened the door wide.
He sauntered through the wrecked assembly hall.
Scared faces turned. Eyes that remembered his bruises

clouded over, younger eyes grew shiny.
Suddenly someone shouted, 'Look, the Bully!
Them liars didn't get him! Three cheers for our Bully!'
Then everyone yelled and stamped: 'Three cheers for
    old Bully!'

Old Bully mounted the stage. How tall he was,
what a lovely speech he made. The big boys lifted him high
and they all stormed into the trembling streets, yelling
'Make way, make way for Old Bully!' And everyone did.

CAROL RUMENS

The Strange Visitor

A woman was sitting at her wheel one night;
 And still she sat, and still she span, and still she wished
   for company.

In came a pair of broad broad soles, and sat down at the
   fireside;
 And still she sat, and still she span, and still she wished
   for company.

In came a pair of small small legs, and sat down on the
   broad broad soles;
 And still she sat, and still she span, and still she wished
   for company.

In came a pair of thick thick knees, and sat down on the
   small small legs;
 And still she sat, and still she span, and still she wished
   for company.

In came a pair of thin thin thighs, and sat down on the
   thick thick knees;
 And still she sat, and still she span, and still she wished
   for company.

In came a pair of huge huge hips, and sat down on the
   thin thin thighs;
 And still she sat, and still she span, and still she wished
   for company.

In came a wee wee waist, and sat down on the
huge huge hips;
And still she sat, and still she span, and still she wished
for company.

In came a pair of broad broad shoulders, and sat down
on the wee wee waist;
And still she sat, and still she span, and still she wished
for company.

In came a pair of small small arms, and sat down on the
broad broad shoulders;
And still she sat, and still she span, and still she wished
for company.

In came a pair of huge huge hands, and sat down on the
small small arms;
And still she sat, and still she span, and still she wished
for company.

In came a small small neck, and sat down on the
broad broad shoulders;
And still she sat, and still she span, and still she wished
for company.

In came a huge huge head, and sat down on the
small small neck.

'How did you get such broad broad feet?' quoth the
                woman.
'Much tramping, much tramping!' (*gruffly*).

'How did you get such small small legs?'
'Aih-h-h!—late—and wee-e-e-moul!' (*whiningly*).
'How did you get such thick thick knees?'
'Much praying, much praying!' (*piously*).

How did you get such thin thin thighs?'
'Aih-h-h!—late—and wee-e-e-moul! (*whiningly*).

'How did you get such big big hips?'
'Much sitting, much sitting!' (*gruffly*).

'How did you get such a wee wee waist?'
'Aih-h-h!—late—and wee-e-e-moul! (*whiningly*).

'How did you get such broad broad shoulders?'
'With carrying broom, with carrying broom!' (*gruffly*).

'How did you get such small small arms?'
'Aih-h-h!—late—and wee-e-e-moul! (*whiningly*).

'How did you get such huge huge hands?'
'Threshing with an iron flail, threshing with an iron
                flail!' (*gruffly*).

'How did you get such a small small neck?'
'Aih-h-h!—late—and wee-e-e-moul! (*pitifully*).

'How did you get such a huge huge head?'
'Much knowledge, much knowledge!' (*keenly*).

'What did you come for?'
'FOR YOU!'

Traditional
chosen by Carol Rumens

YOUR GRANDMOTHER

Remember, remember, there's many a thing
your grandmother doesn't dig
if it ain't got that swing;
many a piece of swag
she won't pick up and put in her bag
if it seems like a drag.
She painted it red – the town –
she lassooed the moon.
Remember, remember, your grandmother
boogied on down.

Remember, remember, although your grandmother's old,
she shook, she rattled, she rolled.
She was so cool she was cold,
she was solid gold.
Your grandmother played it neat,
wore two little blue suede shoes
on her dancing feet –
oo, reet-a-teet-teet –
Remember, remember, your grandmother
got with the beat.

Remember, remember, it ain't what you do
it's the way that you do it.
Your grandmother knew it –
she had a balloon and she blew it,
she had a ball
and was belle of it
just for the hell of it.

She was Queen of the night.
Remember, remember, your grandmother's
aaaaaaaaaaaallllllll riiiiiiiiiiiiiight.

CAROL ANN DUFFY

Overheard on a Saltmarsh

Nymph, nymph, what are your beads?

Green glass, goblin. Why do you stare at them?

Give them me.

      No.

Give them me. Give them me.

          No.

Then I will howl all night in the reeds,
Lie in the mud and howl for them.

Goblin, why do you love them so?

They are better than stars or water,
Better than voices of winds that sing,
Better than any man's fair daughter,
Your green glass beads on a silver ring.

Hush, I stole them out of the moon.

Give me your beads, I want them.

          No.

I will howl in a deep lagoon
For your green glass beads, I love them so.
Give them me. Give them.

                    No.

Harold Monro
chosen by Carol Ann Duffy

Answers to RIDDLES pages 37–38

1. Pasta 2. Hot-water bottle 3. False teeth
4. Door knocker 5.Woodcutter 6. Bed spring
7. Aluminium ladder 8. Nails
9. Dolly mixtures 10. Cadbury's Roses sweets
11. Cadbury's GIANT chocolate bar
12. Washing-up liquid

INDEX OF FIRST LINES

INDEX OF POETS

ACKNOWLEDGEMENTS

The compiler and publishers wish to thank the following for permission to use copyright material:

Hilaire Belloc, 'Tarantella' from *Complete Verse* by Hilaire Belloc, Random House UK, by permission of PFD on behalf of the Estate of the author; Judi Benson, 'The Lucky Ones', by permission of the author; John Betjeman 'Hunter Trials' from *Collected Poems* by John Betjeman, by permission of John Murray (Publishers) Ltd; Sujata Bhatt, 'The Snake Catcher Speaks' from *Augatora* by Sujata Bhatt (2000), by permission of Carcanet Press Ltd; Elizabeth Bishop, 'A Summer's Dream' from *The Complete Poems: 1927–1979* by Elizabeth Bishop. Copyright © 1979, 1983 by Alice Helen Methfessel, by permission of Farrar, Straus and Giroux, LLC; Valerie Bloom, 'Secret', included in *The World is Sweet*, Bloomsbury Children's Books (2000), by permission of the author; George Mackay Brown, 'Hamnavoe Market' from *Selected Poems 1954–1991* by George Mackay Brown, by permission of John Murray (Publishers) Ltd; Charles Causley, 'I Saw a Jolly Hunter' from *Collected Poems* by Charles Causley, Macmillan, by permission of David Higham Associates on behalf of the author; Linda Chase, 'Timing' from *The Wedding Spy* by Linda Chase (2001), by permission of Carcanet Press Ltd; Wendy Cope, 'An Attempt at Unrhymed Verse', by permission of PFD on behalf of the author; E. E. Cummings, 'anyone lived in a pretty how town' from *Complete Poems 1904–1962* by E. E. Cummings, ed. George J Firmage. Copyright © 1991 by the Trustees for the E. E. Cummings Trust and George James Firmage, by permission of W W Norton & Company; Amanda Dalton, 'Touch', by permission of the author; U. A. Fanthorpe, 'The Beasts', by permission of the author; Robert Frost, 'Stopping by Woods on a Snowy Evening' from *The Poetry of Robert Frost*, ed, Edward Connery Latham, Jonathan Cape, by permission The Random House Group Ltd on behalf of the Estate of Robert Frost; Robert Graves, 'Warning to Children' from *Complete Poems* by Robert Graves, by permission of Carcanet Press Ltd; Philip Gross, 'History Lesson' from *The All Nite Cafe* by Philip Gross (1993), by permission of Faber and Faber Ltd; Sophie Hannah, 'The World is a Box', by permission of Carcanet Press Ltd; John Hegley, 'Eddie Don't Like Furniture', by permission of PFD on behalf of the author; Selima Hill, 'Riddles', by permission of the author; Miroslav Holub, 'A Dog in a Quarry' from *Miroslav Holub: Selected Poems*. trs. Ian Milner and George Theiner (1967). Copyright © Miroslav Holub 1967. Translation copyright © Penguin Books, 1967, by permission of Penguin Books Ltd; Libby Houston, 'The Dragonfly' from *Cover of Darkness, Selected Poems 1961–1998* by Libby Houston, Slow Dancer Press. Copyright © Libby Houston 1981, 1999, by permission of the author; Jenny Joseph, 'In a Dark Stone' from *Ghosts and other company*, Bloodaxe Books (1995), by permission of John Johnson (Authors' Agent) Ltd on behalf of the author; Jackie Kay, 'The World of Trees', by permission of the author; Roger McGough, 'The Midnight Skaters' from *Pillow Talk* by Roger McGough, Viking, by permission of PFD on behalf of the author;